UFO's

ROBERT JACKSON

A QUINTET BOOK

ISBN: 0-7858-0499-4

This book was designed and produced by
Quintet Publishing Limited

Creative Director: Richard Dewing
Designer: Nicky Chapman
Project Editor: Stefanie Foster
Editor: Rosemary Booton
Picture Research: Liz Eddison
Jacket Design: Nik Morley

Typeset in Great Britain by
Central Southern Typesetters, Eastbourne

Produced in Australia by Griffin Colour

Published by Chartwell Books
A Division of Book Sales, Inc.
P.O. Box 7100
Edison, New Jersey 08818-7100

Contents

Where it all began

It began with Kenneth Arnold

Kenneth Arnold was by no means the first person to witness the phenomenon nowadays called an Unidentified Flying Object, or UFO, but it was his experience that sparked off the wave of UFO hysteria that was to endure throughout much of the 1950s.

It happened on Tuesday, 24 June 1947. Arnold, a businessman from Boise, Idaho, was flying from Chehalis to Yakima in Washington State, piloting his own aircraft. He had been installing fire-fighting equipment for the Chehalis Central Air Service earlier that afternoon, and had overheard someone

BELOW Kenneth Arnold, the businessman from Boise, Idaho, who sighted something strange in the sky near Mount Rainier on 24 June 1947. It was his experience that sparked off the wave of UFO hysteria that was to endure throughout much of the 1950s.

comment that there was a $5,000 reward for anyone locating the wreckage of a US Marine Corps' C-46 transport, lost somewhere in the Mount Rainier area. The possible crash site was some distance off Arnold's intended route, but he decided to make a short detour into the search area; the reward, after all, was a tempting carrot.

As he cruised along at 9,000 feet (2,743m), a sudden flash of light caught his attention. At first, he thought that another aircraft must be in the vicinity, perhaps also involved in the search for the missing transport. He scanned the sky, but could see no sign of it. Then, as he looked to the north of Mount Rainier, he saw something unusual: nine odd-looking aircraft, flying in line astern at 9,500 feet (2,869m) and following a heading of 170 degrees. Every few seconds, two or three of them would dip or change their course slightly, just enough for the sun to catch their reflective surfaces. The strange craft appeared to be crescent-shaped,

with no sign of any tail surfaces. Arnold assumed that they were some new type of jet aircraft. He saw their shape in greater detail as they passed in front of snow-covered Mount Rainier, and now an even bigger surprise was in store; they were not crescent-shaped, but round. They were a long way off – about 25 miles (40km), according to his estimate – and so had to be fairly large, perhaps about the size of a DC-4 airliner, in order to be visible. They were also fast. Using the second hand of his wrist-watch, Arnold timed the passage of the discs over a known distance between Mount Rainier and another mountain peak. His initial calculations indicated that the craft were flying at 1,700mph (2,735kmh) – an unheard-of speed for any aircraft in 1947. Even later, when more precise calculations were made, their speed could not be reduced below 1,300mph (2,092kmh).

On landing, Arnold decided to report what he had seen to the FBI, but the local office was closed.

ABOVE **Mount Rainier in Washington State provided a majestic backdrop not only for Arnold's UFO sighting, but also for several others in the years that followed. The mountain is a 14,410-ft (4,392-m) dormant volcano.**

"From then on, if I was to go by the number of reports that came in of other sightings, . . . I thought it wouldn't be long before there would be one of these things in every garage."

Instead, he told the media, and the story went out to the world over the wires of the Associated Press. Within hours of its appearance, reports were coming in from all sides from people who claimed to have witnessed similar craft. Arnold himself, besieged by reporters, commented ironically: "From then on, if I was to go by the number of reports that came in of other sightings, of which I kept a close track, I thought it wouldn't be long before there would be one of these things in every garage. In order to stop what I thought was a lot of foolishness, and since I couldn't get any work done, I went out to the airport, cranked up my plane, and flew home to Boise." But the damage had been done. The newspapers now had a blizzard of UFO sightings on their hands, and exploited them to the full. Reporter Bill Begrette coined the term "Flying Saucers".

● **ABOVE** Kenneth Arnold displays a drawing of the crescent-shaped craft he saw in the vicinity of Mount Rainier. After his sighting, the press was deluged with UFO sighting reports from all over the United States.

Investigations begin in America

In January 1948, in the wake of this initial wave of sightings, the US Government launched its first official probe into the UFO phenomenon. These were dangerous times: the "Iron Curtain" had descended across Europe, confrontation between the Soviet Union and the Western allies was escalating, and the Russians were known to be developing long-range bombers capable of flying over the Pole to North America. The Americans themselves were engaged in a highly-secret weapons programme, partly involving the development of a new generation of super-powerful nuclear weapons and rocket missiles. This programme, as far as rocketry was concerned, was being conducted with the aid of German scientists, and the Russians were known to have German scientists working for them too. No one knew how far development had progressed inside the Soviet Union, and speculation arose as to whether the UFOs were in some way connected with it.

To make matters worse, the American public was beginning to grow paranoid about the Soviets. Magazines and newspapers carried fanciful reports, often supported by faked photographs, of amazing new Soviet military aircraft. It was said, for example, that they had flown a piloted rocket plane – based on a wartime German design – that could reach a speed of 1,600mph (2,574kmh) and an altitude of 90,000 feet (27,432m). It seemed

● **LEFT** Fear of military developments in the Soviet Union undoubtedly accounted for part of the UFO hysteria. In the late 1940s the Russians were developing intercontinental bomber prototypes like this Tupolev Tu-85. Its design was based on America's B-29.

form of alien spacecraft was little more than a germ in the minds of most people; admittedly, there had been an "alien invasion" scare in 1939, when an all-too-realistic radio dramatization of H. G. Wells' *The War of the Worlds* had sent a brief ripple of panic across the United States, but that had soon died out in shame-faced fashion. Since then the public had been sceptical about aliens in general.

They were by no means sceptical about what the Russians might be up to, though, and so the US Air Force (USAF), in charge of UFO investigations, devoted much time and effort to providing rational explanations of the phenomenon. They tried to explain them away as weather balloons, atmospheric conditions or the light of planets such as Venus, magnified by layers of the Earth's atmosphere. It was also revealed that the Americans themselves had been experimenting with saucer-shaped aircraft. One of them, the Chance Vought XF5U-1, had been rolled out in 1946. It was the prototype of a carrier-based fighter; but the problem was that it had never flown.

ABOVE Many post-war Russian jet aircraft were produced with the help of captured German scientists. This Ilyushin Il-22, which flew in 1947, drew heavily on wartime German technology – but nothing the Russians had could reach a speed of 1,600mph (2,575kmph) at 90,000 feet (27,432m), despite fanciful rumours.

plausible enough; after all, the Americans themselves had already exceeded the speed of sound with a piloted rocket plane, the Bell X-1, and speeds were being pushed higher all the time.

The US Government's priority, then, was to allay public fears about UFOs, and what they might be. At this stage, the idea that they might be some

RIGHT America's own "flying saucer", the disc-shaped Chance Vought XF5U-1. The prototype of a carrier-based fighter, it was built in 1946 but never flew.

It was the US film industry that implanted the widespread notion that UFOs might be alien spacecraft. It all started in 1951, with the release of a film entitled *The Day the Earth Stood Still*. In this, a flying saucer lands in America, bringing friendly aliens to warn the peoples of Earth against the dangers of modern war. In the following year UFO sightings reached an unprecedented peak – and reports were leaked of sightings by USAF crews, as well as by the general public.

 **L E F T** A moment of terror for actress Patricia Neal in the film *The Day the Earth Stood Still*. The film was released in 1951, was a huge box office success, and in the following year UFO sightings reached an unprecedented peak.

Sighting over the Gulf of Mexico

At 5.25am on 6 December 1952, Lieutenant Sid Coleman was watching the main radar scope of his B-29 bomber, which was flying over the Gulf of Mexico. Suddenly, the blip of an unknown object, followed by two other blips, appeared on the screen. Coleman checked their speed: it was an incredible 5,240mph (8,431kmh). The navigator also reported blips on his scope. By the time Coleman had recalibrated his set, Captain John Harter had also registered four unknowns.

As a blip approached on the right, another crew member, Master Sergeant Bailey, peered into the night and saw a blue-lit object streak from the front to the rear of the bomber. A second group of blips appeared on all three scopes, followed by a third group. Bending over his screen, the radar officer saw two UFOs rocketing by on the right. He alerted Staff Sergeant Ferris, who looked out through the waist blister. Instantly, Ferris saw two objects streak by, mere blurs of blue-white light.

Up in the cockpit, Captain Harter saw the UFOs cut across the bomber's course, an estimated 40 miles (64km) away. Suddenly, they turned and headed straight towards the B-29. Then, abruptly, they slowed to the bomber's speed, turned in behind it and kept pace with it for ten seconds before pulling off to one side. At the same moment, Captain Harter saw a huge half-inch blip on the scope, moving at 5,000mph (8,045kmh). The smaller UFOs increased their speed, merged with the larger one, and instantly the huge blip accelerated to 9,000mph (14,481kmh) before disappearing.

BELOW A Boeing B-29 bomber. On 6 December 1952, the crew of one of these aircraft sighted several UFOs over the Gulf of Mexico. The strange craft shadowed the bomber for several minutes before accelerating away at speeds of up to 9,000mph (14,484kph).

Civilian airline sightings in the US

A few months earlier, on 14 July 1952, there had been another aerial sighting, this time involving a civilian airliner. At 9.12pm, Pan American pilots First Officer W. B. Nash and Second Officer W. H. Fortenberry were approaching Norfolk, Virginia, in their DC-4 when they saw six disc-shaped UFOs ahead. The UFOs, glowing orange-red, were approaching at fantastic speed in echelon formation. The first disc slowed abruptly, just as if someone – or something – inside it had sighted the DC-4. The next two discs wobbled for an instant, seeming almost to overrun the leader, and then all six suddenly flipped up on edge, changed course violently and streaked away.

The two pilots watched as the discs returned to their flat position, and lined up again in echelon formation. A second afterwards, two other discs raced under the DC-4 and joined the six ahead. Suddenly, all the UFOs went dark. When their glow reappeared, all eight machines were in line. Then they climbed away rapidly and vanished.

A week later, in the Air Traffic Control Center at Washington National Airport, controller Ed Nugent saw seven sharp blips suddenly appear on the main radar scope. He called the tower, where radar operator Howard Cocklin confirmed that he also had blips on his scope. Later, another controller, Jim Ritchey, saw that a UFO was pacing a Capital airliner that had just taken off. He called the captain, a veteran pilot named "Casey" Pierman, and asked him to investigate. Until then, the UFO's tracked speed had been about 130mph (209kmh). Then, abruptly, it stopped tracking the aircraft. A moment later, Pierman radioed that he had seen the thing, but that it had streaked off before he had been able to get close to it.

● BELOW A DC-4 airliner similar to the one that encountered UFOs over Virginia on 14 July 1952. The UFOs approached the aircraft at fantastic speed before slowing down, changing course and streaking away.

Trying to explain the phenomenon

The fact that UFOs could be tracked by radar was clear proof that whatever they were, they were solid. The inference was that they were real, and that they could not be explained away as natural phenomena. Often, as in the case of the B-29 crew,

radar contacts were confirmed by visual sightings. This happened again on 5 August 1952, when personnel at the USAF base at Oneida, Japan, saw a UFO carrying a bright white light approaching their base. Watching from the control tower, they made out a dark circular shape behind the glow, about four times the diameter of the light. A smaller, less brilliant light shone from the round, dark under-surface of the strange craft. For several minutes it hovered near the tower, its dark shape clearly visible behind the light, then it accelerated away.

The peak month for UFO sightings in 1952 was April, when at least 100 well-documented reports were made in the USA and Canada. Some of these undoubtedly involved missile tests and fast, high-flying jet aircraft; with the Korean War in full swing the USAF was carrying out a great deal of experi-

● LEFT In the early 1950s, the USAF was carrying out a great deal of experimental flying. Here, an F-84 fighter links up with a B-36 bomber in a long range fighter escort experiment. Could such activities account for sightings of "UFOs joining up with their mother ships"?

Not a massive flying saucer, but a lenticular cloud formation pictured over Eastern Bohemia. The cloud is formed above a mountain ridge when the wind blows in the direction of the mountain slopes.

INSETS **The cover of the second issue of *Fate* magazine, summer 1948, featuring UFOs. The UFO phenomenon allowed artists to exercise their imaginations to the ultimate degree. Ten years later, the same artistic licence was still running strong. This edition of *Fate* magazine, February 1958, depicts yet another UFO sighting.**

mental flying during this period, including in-flight refuelling at night. The aircraft involved, flying high, would display clusters of lights that might appear strange to an uninitiated observer on the ground. Many of the reports also stated that the UFO alternately showed red, green and white lights as it changed position in the sky; the navigation lights of an aircraft are red at the port wingtip, green at the starboard, and white at the tail. Nevertheless, the majority of UFO sightings could not be explained away so easily, and by the end of 1952 the phenomenon was well established throughout the world. Flying-saucer research groups sprang up everywhere, and sightings multiplied in countries other than the United States. With this massive wave of interest, there arose a lamentable tendency to invent UFO stories, or at least to seize on historical events and attempt to "prove" that alien activity had somehow been involved. Eagerly, in their search for evidence of alien contact in past ages, UFO devotees turned their attention to the world's ancient records – in particular the Bible. From now on, UFOs and religion were to follow a closely parallel path.

Shot down by UFOs?

The mystery of McChord Air Force Base, Tacoma

At 6.30pm on 1 April 1959, a big four-engined C-118 transport aircraft of the USAF's 1705th Air Transport Wing roared down the main runway of McChord Air Force Base, near Tacoma, Washington, and climbed away into the southern sky. For the four-man crew, this was a routine training mission – so routine that it was virtually automatic. But just 75 minutes later, all four men were dead – and the C-118 was a mass of shredded wreckage strewn across the side of a mountain.

"Mayday, Mayday! We've hit something – or something has hit us . . . This is it! This is it!"

At 7.45pm, the staff in the control tower at McChord Air Base heard a frantic distress call from the C-118's pilot. "Mayday, Mayday! We've hit something – or something has hit us . . . This is it!" Then there was only silence. The C-118 had crashed into the side of a mountain in the Cascade Range, 30 miles (48km) north-west of Mount Rainier's 14,400ft (4,389m) peak. Air Force crash crews and armed guards raced to the scene and threw a cordon around the widely scattered wreckage. Newsmen and others who attempted to come close

BELOW A Douglas C-118 military transport aircraft. On 1 April, 1959, an aircraft of this type was destroyed under mysterious circumstances in the Cascade Mountains, not far from Mount Rainier. What brought it down remains a mystery to this day.

were warned off at gunpoint. Explanations and rumours spread like wildfire. Had the aircraft been testing some new device – hence all the secrecy? Unlikely, as the C-118 was only a freighter. Was pilot error the answer? Or perhaps the C-118 had run into a flock of birds, or had been in collision with a second aircraft.

The Air Force knew that none of these reasons was the real one. A few minutes before the pilot's distress call, the powerful radars at McChord Air Base had revealed that the C-118 had picked up three or four mysterious travelling companions – strange, luminous peaks of light that darted around the big transport. Gradually, the Air Force specialists who were investigating the crash began to build up a minute-by-minute picture of the strange and terrifying fate that had overwhelmed the aircraft and its crew.

At seven o'clock on that April evening, residents in the area between Seattle and Mount Rainier had been alarmed by a series of explosions – mysterious detonations that seemed to come from a clear sky. Twenty minutes later, the whole region was shaken by an even bigger bang. At about the same time, several bright, luminous objects were seen racing across the sky. They travelled at incredible speed and in complete silence. Many other people witnessed strange flashes and glows around the horizon.

Eye-witnesses in Orting, not far from the scene of the crash, told investigators that the C-118 had appeared overhead at about 7.45pm. All the aircraft's four engines were stopped, and a large chunk of its tail unit was missing. But, strangest of all, the C-118 was being followed by a formation of three shining discs. Every now and then, one of them would break away and dart towards the transport, skipping over it and veering off to one side at the last moment. It was just as though the C-118 was being harried by a pack of hounds. Several people in the Orting area had watched the aircraft and its unearthly companions until they were out of sight. A minute later, two bright flashes ripped the sky to the north-east. At that exact moment the radio transmissions from the C-118 ceased abruptly with the pilot's final desperate "This is it!"

Rescue teams arriving at the scene of the crash found a nightmare of charred, twisted metal fragments, hardly any of them more than a foot across, scattered over the whole mountainside. They found three mangled, dislocated bodies, too, sunk deep

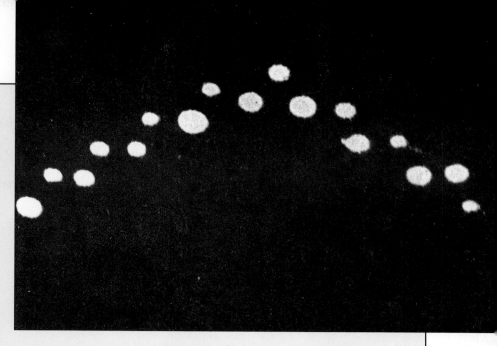

into the ground by the fearful impact. The fourth body, however, was never found. The aircraft's tail-fin and rudder were discovered much later, miles away in the hills to the north of Mount Rainier.

From the wilderness of torn wreckage, the accident investigators were able to reconstruct exactly how the C-118 had hit the ground, and they came up with a number of facts that baffled them completely. For a start, they calculated that even if the aircraft had nose-dived into the ground under full power, the impact would not have been great enough to rip the machine into such a widely scattered sea of small fragments. But the C-118 had not ploughed into the earth nose-first; it had struck on its belly, as though something had swatted it out of the sky with enormous force.

Whatever conclusions the US Air Force reached, it kept quiet about them, and did its best to lay a smoke screen over the incident. The uncanny story behind the crash first came to light several weeks later, when investigators from a civilian research group known as the Aerial Phenomena Research Organization – which specializes in gathering information on UFO sightings and related incidents – arrived on the scene. Their report was published in May 1959, and caused a few red faces in the USAF's Information Bureau.

Just what really did happen in those last fateful minutes before the C-118's plunge to earth will never be known. There are all sorts of rational explanations for what might have caused the crash; extreme turbulence and "wind shear", which can smack an aircraft out of the sky without warning, are just two. But there can be no rational explanation for the silver discs that seemed to be harrying the C-118 to its destruction.

ABOVE The unfortunate C-118 was shadowed by luminous discs like those in this picture. This photograph was taken on 30 August 1951 by Carl Hart Jr. as the UFOs passed over Texas.

The Kentucky incident

BELOW Captain Thomas Mantell, Jr, was asked to investigate the strange UFO over Kentucky on 7 January 1948. He climbed in pursuit of it – and minutes later he was dead.

It was in the Mount Rainier area that Kenneth Arnold had seen his strange circular craft skipping around the mountain peaks in 1947, but it was on the other side of the American continent, on 7 January 1948, that another incident occurred which foreshadowed the fate of the C-118 by 11 years. The setting for the January 1948 incident was Kentucky. All day long, the townspeople of Marysville, Irvington and Owensboro and the villages in between had been reporting sightings of a big,

shining UFO, moving slowly and silently across the sky. At 1.15pm, the Chief of Police in Marysville, his office overwhelmed by calls, rang nearby Godman Air Force Base to see if he could obtain any information on the strange phenomenon. The senior air traffic controller at Godman in turn telephoned the Air Force Test Center at Wright-Patterson Field, and was assured that no aircraft of any kind was being tested in the area round Godman Field and Marysville. At 1.35pm, Godman's radar scanners locked on to an "unidentified aircraft" that was approaching the airfield from the south-east at a height of about 13,000 feet (3,962m). Ten minutes later, the controllers picked up the object visually, and saw at once that it was no ordinary aircraft. The thing was shining and circular. It was difficult to estimate its actual size, but it appeared to be about 500 feet (150m) in diameter. It drifted over the centre of the airfield and then stopped, hanging motionless just below the cloud base.

The sky was covered with a layer of cirrostratus (ie uniform) cloud at 14,000 feet (4,270m), through which the sun shone with a pale light. After half an hour, the mystery object shot upwards a few hundred feet until it entered the cloud base. It continued to lurk there, visible now as a hazy, dull-red glow. In the control tower, a heated discussion was going on between the controllers, the base commander, the operations officer, the intelligence officer and several others. They all agreed on one point: the thing up there was not an aircraft or a weather balloon.

At 2.30pm, Godman Tower received a call from the leader of a flight of five P-51 Mustang fighters. They were on a ferry flight, and were about to overfly the field. Godman asked the flight leader, Captain Thomas Mantell, if he would investigate the UFO. At that time, the Mustang flight was about 10 miles south of Godman, and was flying below the cloud base.

Mantell acknowledged, and informed Godman Tower that he was turning on to a heading of 220 degrees and climbing to 15,000 feet (4,570m) in order to intercept the mystery craft. As they passed through 15,000 feet (4,570m), two of the Mustang pilots suddenly broke away and descended. These

■ ABOVE A North
American F-51D Mustang
fighter similar to the one
Captain Mantell was flying
when he met his death.
Many of the stories
surrounding the crash are
pure myth, as are the last
words allegedly spoken by
the pilot.

aircraft were not carrying oxygen equipment, which in accordance with USAF regulations was mandatory for flights above 14,000 feet (4,270m). Mantell's Mustang was not fitted with oxygen gear either, but he continued to climb, accompanied by the remaining two pilots, Lieutenant A. W. Clements and Lieutenant B. A. Hammond. Their Mustangs both had oxygen, but at 22,000 feet (6,700m) Hammond's supply began to fail and he too broke

> **"Jesus Christ, it's fantastic! It's right above me, and it's tremendous! It looks metallic, and it's huge and circular. It could be anything between 500 and 1,000 feet across. It seems to be cruising at about 200 knots, and I'm gaining on it. It's colossal! I'm going to try and get above it. It's climbing! It's starting to climb . . . God, this is fantastic! It's getting hot. It's hot! The heat! I can't . . ."**

away, followed by Clements. Both continued to track the UFO at a lower altitude while Mantell went up to 23,000 feet (7,000m).

At this point, Mantell allegedly radioed: "Jesus Christ, it's fantastic! It's right above me, and it's tremendous! It looks metallic, and it's huge and circular. It could be anything between 500 and a 1,000 feet across. It seems to be cruising at about 200 knots, and I'm gaining on it. It's colossal! I'm going to try and get above it. It's climbing! It's starting to climb . . . God, this is fantastic! It's getting hot. It's hot! The heat! I can't . . ." And then, so the story goes, there was silence.

In fact, Captain Mantell said nothing of the sort. His words were the invention of dozens of lurid newspaper stories that appeared in the wake of the incident. He did say that he had sighted the UFO, that it was above and ahead of him and appeared to be moving at about half his speed, and that it was large and metallic. After that, there were no further transmissions from him. The other Mustang pilots, following the course of the UFO at a safe oxygen level below the cloud, could see neither the object nor their leader. They had tried to warn him about the danger of flying too high without oxygen, but had received no response.

At about 3.15pm, Captain Mantell's Mustang dived vertically into a field on a farm near Franklin, Kentucky, and exploded in a cloud of debris. His body was found in what was left of the cockpit. Some later reports suggested that the remains of the aircraft were "pitted and scored by intense heat", implying that the Mustang had been destroyed by some kind of death ray. Like the spurious contents of the radio transmission, that was not true either; and a post-mortem examination of Mantell's body showed that he had been killed on impact, not earlier.

By the evening, newspapers all over the country had got hold of the story of Mantell's strange and final experience, and the US Air Force felt compelled to issue a statement. The official line was that Mantell, a highly experienced pilot (he was not a fighter "ace", as some reports claimed, but had flown transport aircraft during the war) had been killed when his P-51 exceeded its airframe's structural limits and broke up in mid-air. And the mystery object he had been chasing? Nothing more than the planet Venus, magnified by atmospheric conditions. Astronomers all over the world were no doubt interested to learn that the planet Venus could be picked up by ordinary airfield radar, that it was metallic, up to 1,000 feet (305m) in diameter, and cruised at 200 knots 15,000 feet (4,570m) above the earth. Apparently realizing just how ludicrous this explanation was, the Air Force issued another. This time, they said that Mantell had flown into a meteorological balloon. A weather balloon that cruised around at will all over Kentucky, that hung motionless over an airfield for nearly an hour in spite of high winds at altitude, and then suddenly vanished? Nevertheless, despite all the stories, the weather balloon still remains the official Air Force explanation.

BELOW The USAF tried to explain the Mantell crash by saying that the pilot had been chasing the planet Venus, magnified by atmospheric conditions. Another "explanation" was that he had flown into a weather balloon.

A B O V E Is this aircraft being shadowed by a UFO? The photograph, taken in September 1957, shows a Martin B-57 jet bomber apparently being followed by a mystery object. The UFO (arrowed) did not show up up until the film was developed.

So what really happened to Captain Mantell? The logical answer is that he suffered anoxia – oxygen starvation – and passed out. The process takes only a few seconds, and the unfortunate aspect is that the afflicted pilot does not realize it

"My intentions are to go to King Island . . . That strange aircraft is hovering on top of me again. It is hovering and it's not an aircraft. Delta Sierra Juliet, Melbourne . . ."

is happening. His aircraft then went out of control, and crashed before he regained consciousness. But what was he chasing over Kentucky that day? That will forever remain a mystery. It must have been something very, very important to make Captain Mantell ignore his years of Air Force training and be oblivious to his own safety. However, the secret of what he really encountered died with him.

So did the secret of what Australian pilot Frederick Valentich saw on 21 October 1978, during

what were apparently the last minutes of his life. Twenty-year-old Valentich was flying a Cessna 182 from Melbourne's Moorabbin Airport to King Island, off the coast of Victoria, when he encountered what at first sight seemed to be a large aircraft flying over Bass Strait a few minutes after seven o'clock in the evening.

It was soon apparent that the object was not an aircraft. Metallic and shining, and showing what Valentich described as a green light to Melbourne Air Traffic Control, it buzzed his Cessna at high speed and then hovered overhead.

Valentich told Melbourne that his engine was beginning to run roughly. Melbourne asked him what his intentions were. "My intentions are to go to King Island . . . That strange aircraft is hovering on top of me again. It is hovering and it's not an aircraft. Delta Sierra Juliet, Melbourne . . ."

And that was all. After that last transmission, Frederick Valentich and his Cessna, callsign Delta Sierra Juliet, simply vanished. No trace of either was ever found.

Strange things in Earth orbit

The mystery satellite of the North and South Poles

The discovery, when it was made, caused consternation in the United States Defense Department; and no wonder. One of the North American Air Defense System's tracking radars had picked up what appeared to be a huge space satellite in orbit around the earth.

What worried the Americans was that the satellite had not been launched by either the United States or the Soviet Union. For a start, it was in the wrong kind of orbit. The mystery satellite's path took it over the North and South Poles, whereas the orbits of satellites launched from the Soviet Union were invariably inclined at 65 degrees to the equator, which took them over South America and North Africa. Quite apart from that, there was no booster rocket in existence at the time – February 1960 – that could possibly have been powerful enough to put such a satellite into orbit. American space scientists had calculated that its weight was around 15 tons (15.25 tonnes). For three weeks, the Americans kept the satellite under surveillance; then it vanished, as mysteriously as it had appeared.

● **BELOW** Earth – the home of all mankind. This fantastic view of our home planet was taken by the crew of the Apollo 17 spacecraft during the final lunar landing mission in the Apollo programme. The scope of the photograph extends from the Mediterranean Sea to Antarctica.

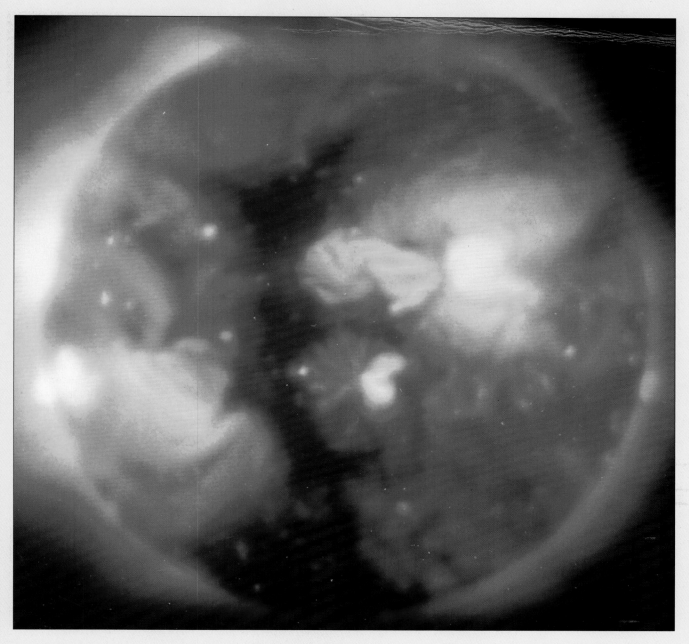

● **ABOVE** **This picture of the sun was taken by the Solar Telescope of Skylab. First seen in X-ray pictures, scores of bright points of light dot the solar disc, like scattered jewels. The glittering points are found all over the sun.**

The "mystery satellite" of February 1960 was the first in a whole series of strange space phenomena which have been baffling scientists all over the world for three decades. On 3 September 1960, seven months after the first sighting, it was revealed that an unidentified object had been photographed in the sky over New York by a tracking camera at the Grumman Aircraft Corporation's Long Island factory. The object, which appeared to give off a reddish glow, had been seen several times during the preceding two weeks. It was apparently follow-ing an east-to-west orbit, whereas most satellites were launched in the opposite direction, and its speed appeared to be about three times that of America's Echo 1 "metal balloon" satellite.

The Americans attached so much importance to these mystery satellites that they set up a special committee to gather as much information as possible about them. But the committee's findings – if indeed there were any at all – were never made public, and the whole affair was forgotten for the time being.

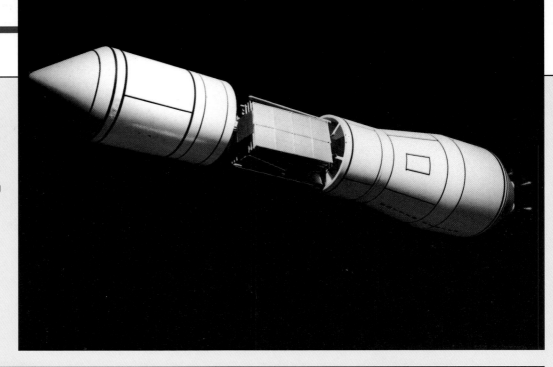

● RIGHT The Pegasus satellite on the final stage of its booster rocket. This was what the USAF said White and McDivitt had seen – but it was over 1,000 miles (1,600km) away at the time.

Strange activities in the Soviet Union

● RIGHT Lt Cdr James Lovell who, with Frank Borman, also sighted an unidentified object in orbit during their record-breaking 14-day Gemini flight around the world. It may have been a secret military reconnaissance satellite.

There may have been a rational explanation for all the sightings in the US. There was certainly one behind waves of UFO hysteria that gripped certain parts of the Soviet Union in the 20 years or so before *Glasnost*.

In June 1980, for example, a great crescent-shaped UFO streaked over the skies of central Russia, glowing bright red. It was seen by hundreds of thousands of people, many of whom panicked in the belief that American nuclear rockets were descending on them. In the days that followed, the mysterious object received a lot of press coverage in the USSR. Some of the more way-out pseudo-scientific journals – of which there are quite a number in Russia – even hinted that aliens had been seen in the streets of Moscow and other Soviet cities.

But it wasn't just the Russians who saw the strange object. An hour later, it was sighted by people in Chile, Argentina, Brazil and Uruguay – still crescent-shaped, but apparently much smaller now and not glowing so brightly. By now, the object was being tracked by the big radar scanners of the United States Air Defense Command, and they showed it up for what it really was. The thing that had terrified half the population of the central Soviet Union was nothing more than a Cosmos military reconnaissance satellite – or rather, the rocket that launched it.

LT CDR JAMES LOVELL

The RD-107 booster rockets that launch Russia's military satellites consist of 20 rocket engines, strapped around a central body to provide a massive initial thrust and acceleration. Once this has been achieved, the boosters are jettisoned and stage two takes over, increasing the acceleration to orbital velocity. When they are all firing together, the clusters of rocket motors that surround the base of

Dazzling UFOs which lit up the night skies over Honduras have been linked by experts to two mystifying power blackouts which plunged the capital city into darkness.

Hundreds of eyewitnesses — including government officials — were terrified by the strange glowing objects.

And a Honduran professor openly admits he believes the power losses are due to a "controlled force" that could have come from "extraterrestrial life."

On Oct. 14, 1978, a bizarre boomerang-shaped UFO was sighted swooping through the sky only a few seconds before power was knocked out for 25 minutes.

Just two weeks later, on October 27, a brilliant, octopus-shaped UFO appeared — and the sightings of this strange craft also coincided with a massive electricity failure of 1 hour and 10 minutes.

The Honduran government officially attributes the power losses to children's kites getting tangled in the power lines. But many people — even some in government — scoff at that theory.

"That's absurd," snorted Dr. Salvador Pardo, dean of the school of engineering at the National and Autonomous University of Honduras. "Kites could not have caused this damage.

"The power went out and then came back — without repairs," he stressed. "This to me makes it obvious that a controlled force caused this blackout. It is perfectly logical to assume that extraterrestrial life could have caused the blackouts."

Added Lieut. Alexander Her-

By MEL LUNA

nandez, commandant of the Police Officers Academy at Tegucigalpa, the capital city:

"The kite theory is a joke. I personally have seen UFOs in the past here."

Prof. Jose Bercian, director of the program for technical education for the Honduran government, told The ENQUIRER that he, too, had seen a UFO — on September 26.

"What appears to me is that a UFO swept down the high tension lines for whatever reasons and sucked up the power," he said.

As for his own encounter, Prof. Bercian added that while driving at about 2 a.m. September 26, he and his wife had spotted a "glowing globe" that descended rapidly and landed just off the road. "I slowed down and wanted to take a close look," he recalled. "But my wife was terrified and wouldn't let me."

Major Honduran newspapers and TV and radio stations have

SHE SAW IT: Donatila Hernandez Majan points to where UFO hovered over substation.

BERCIAN   LOPEZ   AGUILERA

been flooded with hundreds of reports of UFO sightings dating all the way back to September.

Radio America, one of the country's most popular radio stations, received as many as 200 calls the night of October 27.

"All described the object in exactly the same manner — an octopus-like object showing a brilliant light," commented Radio America news director Rodrigo Wong.

The first blackout, on October 14, was linked to a very different UFO.

"I noticed a V-shaped or boomerang-like object hovering over the airport about a kilometer (half a mile) away at an altitude of 500 meters (1,650 feet)," remembered Rogelio Bercian, director of publicity for La Tribuna, and a brother of Prof. Bercian.

"Suddenly I saw the UFO dive over the airport at an incredible speed and the entire city went black. I later saw this object soaring up in figure-eight maneuvers before it disappeared."

But even more spectacular was the incredible glowing ob-

ject with tentacles of blinding light that coincided with the power outage of two weeks later.

"It looked like an octopus with moving tentacles," remembered taxi driver Roberto Aguilar. "As it swept down into the valley — boom! — all the lights went out."

Herman Badgette, press secretary to the Honduran military junta, was standing on the terrace of the Maya hotel in downtown Tegucigalpa with Associated Press correspondent Tom Fenton.

"I saw a large, bright ball of light," Badgette remembered. "From the white center of the object, multicolored rays of light descended downward.

"Some were blue and red. They looked like bolts of lightning. It disappeared at great speed."

Jorge Alberto Aguilera,

---

the launch vehicle produce an odd effect. Instead of the long ribbon of fire that trails in the wake of America's space boosters, the Russian hardware produces a brilliant crescent-shaped flame that pours from the rocket exhausts as the launcher thunders into the sky.

This is what the Russians saw on that night in June 1980, following the launch of the Cosmos satellite – one of 17 launched that year – from Kapustin Yar, north of the Caspian Sea. The booster rocket's north-east trajectory, inclined at 71 degrees to the equator, took it over Sverdlovsk and across the vast wastes of Siberia. What the peoples of South America saw, an hour later, was probably the second stage of the launch vehicle re-entering the atmosphere and burning up.

For years, flying saucer scares were carefully fostered in the Soviet Union by the state security organization, the KGB, to divert attention from what was really happening in so-called "sensitive areas". For example, anything unusual seen in the skies around Sverdlovsk – a town barred to all foreign visitors because it is an important centre of missile production – was attributed to UFO activity.

● **ABOVE** Late in 1978, a series of dazzling UFOs appeared in the night sky over Honduras, in Central America. They are said to have caused mysterious power blackouts. Could they have been connected with Russian satellite launches?

● **LEFT** A massive solar flare erupting from the sun. The white dot to the right of the photograph represents the Earth, shown to the same scale. Such flares release a cosmic ray bombardment that can produce curious phenomena in the Earth's upper atmosphere.

Lights in the sky

The night of 11 January 1966, was bitterly cold. Patrolman George Dykman pulled up the collar of his fur-lined jacket and shivered as he gazed out across the frozen six-mile (9.6km) expanse of Wanaque Reservoir in New Jersey, 50 miles (80km) from New York. Despite the cold, Dykman had to admit that the scene was peaceful. No sound disturbed the silence, and reflections of starlight glimmered on the reservoir's icy surface.

BELOW Mysterious green fireballs depicted on the front cover of *Fate* magazine, June 1957.

Mystery of the GREEN FIREBALLS

TRUE STORIES OF THE STRANGE AND THE UNKNOWN

FATE MAGAZINE

June 1957 35c

FRANK EDWARDS: The Plot to Silence

Suddenly, something caught Dykman's attention. At first, he thought that it was an aircraft; but then he watched in amazement as the object grew in size, turning into a brilliant white light. It was flying very slowly, cruising over the northern end of the dam. As he watched, its colour turned to red and then to green, and finally back to white again. Dykman had seen enough. Running back to his car, he switched on the radio and alerted other reservoir police patrols. Within minutes, several of his colleagues had arrived on the scene and were gaping in astonishment at the glowing thing that still hovered above the ice.

Other witnesses had seen the strange object, too. They included the Mayor of Wanaque, Harry Wolfe, his 14-year-old son Billy and two members of the city council. Soon, a crowd of people had gathered on the banks of the reservoir. The "craft" shone with a reddish light now, and was cruising backwards and forwards just above the ice. As far as the watchers could estimate, the object was about 10 feet (3m) in diameter. It shone with a constant, unwinking glow, and moved in a curious swaying flight rather like a pendulum.

Abruptly, the object climbed a few hundred feet and became stationary. From it, a brilliant beam of light – like a searchlight, only much thinner – flashed down onto the ice. The light continued to flash on and off at intervals for the next hour. Then, without warning, the object began to gather speed and climbed steeply. A minute late, it was lost among the stars. The crowd of people was just beginning to disperse when more cars roared up, filled with newspaper reporters and photographers. A few of them continued to hang around hopefully for another couple of hours, but at about 1.30am they packed up their gear and went away, bitterly disappointed. Only two policemen, brothers Joe and Dave Cisco, were left to watch the spot.

Just 30 minutes later they radioed that the mysterious light was back again and that they were watching it through binoculars. It looked different this time, like several brilliant stars clustered together in a tight group. After a few minutes it darted away and they lost sight of it.

Early the next morning, reservoir officials went out to inspect the ice. At the northern end of the reservoir, at the spot over which the UFO had hovered, they found that the water was welling up through a number of near-circular holes. It was as if they had been melted through the ice by a huge blowtorch. During the nights that followed, mysterious glowing objects were sighted over and around Wanaque several times. Their colours ranged from white to a brilliant blue, and witnesses reported objects either circular or egg-shaped.

● **ABOVE** This UFO, a luminous disc, was photographed over Paris, France, at 3.45am on 29 December 1953 by engineer Paul Paulin. During the two-minute exposure, the UFO "jumped" sideways and then became stationary again.

The next major sighting occurred in March, when a low-flying UFO terrified nuns at Saint Francis Convent, not far from Wanaque. There were several sightings throughout that summer, but it was not until October 1966 that the UFOs returned to Wanaque Reservoir in force. On 12 October, at least 10 people saw a "flying saucer" hovering over the reservoir. It was like a flat disc, with a rounded dome on top, and seemed to be made of some kind of metal that resembled aluminium. It was first sighted by Sergeant Thompson, a reservoir police officer, who was so startled by the object's brilliant light that he almost drove his car into a tree. The UFO came down low enough over the reservoir to stir up the water in its wake.

By this time, the story was making headlines all over America. Wild theories were put forward to account for the UFO's apparent interest in the reservoir; someone suggested that the waters of reservoirs all over the world were being systematically doped with tranquillizing drugs, so that the Earth could be taken over by invaders from space without a fight. Another theory was that the UFOs actually had a base beneath the waters of Wanaque.

Towards the end of 1966, besieged by a flood of enquiries from all quarters, officials at Stewart Air Force Base near New York issued an explanation. The mysterious flying objects of Wanaque, they said, were nothing more than brightly lit-helicopters. A few days later, apparently realizing just how ridiculous this explanation must have sounded to those who witnessed the UFOs, the Air Force came up with another gem – a standard old faithful, this time. The lights, they said, were the planet Venus. As one of the reservoir policemen told reporters, when the planet Venus comes close enough to stir up the waters of a reservoir in North America, it's time for everyone to start worrying.

● BELOW These mysterious lights in the sky were photographed by a coastguard at Salem, Massachusetts, Air Station in August 1952. He watched them for several seconds as they dimmed and brightened in what appeared to be a regular pattern. The lights were also seen by several colleagues.

RIGHT The silver object in this picture was photographed over Bulawayo in what was then Southern Rhodesia (now Zimbabwe) on 29 December 1953 – the same day that a similar phenomenon was seen over Paris.

An unearthly power in Sweden

Several years before the Wanaque incident, on 20 December 1958, two young Swedes allegedly had an unnerving experience with mysterious, unearthly lights. Stig Rydberg and Hans Gustafsson were driving home through dense fog to spend Christmas with their families when, on a stretch of main road between Hoganas and Helsingborg, they saw a strange, pulsating light among the trees that lined their route. Puzzled, Rydberg pulled the car over to the side of the road and stopped. The two men decided to investigate. Shivering in the chill dampness of the fog, they left the car and began to walk cautiously through the trees towards the weird light.

Suddenly, the men stopped short as a strange, frightening sight met their eyes. In a clearing, a glimmering, diffuse light hovered a few feet above the ground. It seemed to surround a vague, indistinct object. The next instant, the men recoiled in terror. Drifting rapidly towards them, out of the glow, came a cluster of what could only be described as "blobs". They were about three feet (one metre) across, and they gave off an "alien" grey-blue light. Before the two men could move, the blobs were all around them. Gustafsson cried out in fear as a sudden terrifying pressure seized them. Slowly, step by step, an unseen force began to push them towards the pulsating glow.

The two men retched as a frightful stench enveloped them. It was like burnt meat. Rydberg flailed his arms desperately, lashing out at the hovering blobs. His hand plunged deeply into one of them; it was like hitting a quivering jelly. Abruptly, a thin whistling noise split the air. It grew in intensity until the men clasped their hands over their ears in pain. The sound seemed to tear at the very fibre of their brains, destroying their will to resist.

Suddenly Gustafsson stumbled against something, the shock jolting him back to his full senses. It was a post, the remains of an old fence. He grabbed it with both hands and hung on grimly. At once, the terrible force exerted even greater power. To his utter horror, Gustafsson felt his feet rising from the ground. Within seconds he was stretched out

horizontally, his legs waving in mid-air and pointing towards the glowing object. He gritted his teeth and clenched his hands still more firmly around the post.

The force seemed to be concentrating on Gustafsson, and suddenly Rydberg found the pressure lifted from him. He turned and ran towards the car. Looking over his shoulder in fear, he saw that two of the blobs were drifting after him. Branches whipped at his face as he ran as fast as he could through the fog. Reaching the car the now frantic Rydberg tore open the door and jabbed his hand down on the horn.

The sudden harsh blare had an astonishing effect on the blobs. For an instant they wavered, and then they began to drift back towards the glowing thing in the clearing. Gustafsson – still clinging desperately and horizontally to his fence-post – fell to the ground with a thud. Scrambling up, he

● **BELOW LEFT** This drifting luminous disc was photographed by Christian Lynggaard at Vaerlose Air Force Base, Denmark. The photo is quite genuine.

● **BELOW RIGHT** When Mr M. R. Lyons of Nottingham, England, developed the film he had taken in the Derbyshire Peak District in the early summer of 1972 he got a surprise – this ball of hazy light a few inches in diameter appeared on it. He had seen nothing at the time.

stumbled towards the road through the undergrowth and hurled himself into the car.

Trembling with shock and fear, Rydberg started the engine, eager to put as much distance as possible between himself and the terrifying thing in the forest. As he did so, a shrill whining sound cut through the fog. Slowly at first, the pulsating glow in the trees began to rise. Then, gathering speed, it shot upwards until its light was lost in the murk.

It wasn't until three days later that the two young Swedes told anyone about their horrifying experience. They had agreed to keep quiet about it for the simple reason that people would have said that they were either drunk or crazy. But try as they might, they could not shake off the frightful stench that had almost overpowered them in the forest. It clung to them, seeming to grow even stronger as

the days went by, making their stomachs heave with sickness. As last, in desperation, they went to see a doctor. The doctor could find nothing wrong with them, but they were so obviously distressed that he urged them to make a full statement about their experience. During the next few days they were interrogated and examined by police, Swedish defence officials and psychiatrists. None of their interviewers seemed entirely convinced that the two men were telling the truth – until they were subjected to deep hypnosis.

Finally, Rydberg and Gustafsson offered to take the defence experts to the place where they had seen the thing in the clearing. They found no spacecraft and no flying blobs of jelly, but they did find three deep marks in the soft ground, apparently made by some sort of landing gear. The experts examined the area, made notes, and then stamped "Unexplained" on the case file. And, except in the nightmares of two young men, the whole business was forgotten.

● **ABOVE AND RIGHT UFO photographed by Hannah McRoberts north of Kelsey Bay, Vancouver Island, British Columbia, Canada in October 1981. She was photographing the mountain, and neither she nor her companions saw the UFO. The second photograph is a section of the original, concentrating on the mystery object.**

Have UFOs been caught?

Silence over Spitzbergen

The pilot of the Norwegian Air Force Catalina flying boat was bored. For over four hours now, as the aircraft droned deeper into the long Arctic shadows, he and his crew had seen nothing but a vast expanse of grey sea and white ice-floes, lit only by an occasional flash of dim, sunlight that lent a delicate shade of pink to the great ice-pack off Norway's North Cape.

It was May 1952, and the Catalina was on a routine ice-survey mission from its base in northern Norway. Ahead of the aircraft now, and to the right, the jagged snow-capped peaks of Spitzbergen rose

● BELOW The military in the United States and other countries spent a great deal of time and effort searching for UFOs that were reported to have crashed. This cover of *Fate* magazine, May 1954, depicts such a search.

SPECIAL SAUCER ISSUE

FATE MAGAZINE

May 1954
35¢

HUNT FOR THE SAUCERS

A DOCTOR HEALS BY FAITH   I KNEW A WITCH

from the icy sea. The pilot turned the Catalina slightly, bringing it over the island's western shores. Dwarfed by the mountains that towered above it, the aircraft cruised on. Another half an hour or so, and it would be time to set course for home. Suddenly, a flash of reflected light caught the pilot's eye. There was something down there, glittering among the crags. Skimming past a sheer mountain wall, the pilot brought the Catalina down for a closer look. Whatever had caught his attention appeared to be metallic. The long polar shadows made it difficult to make out the exact shape of the object, but it looked like the crumpled wreckage of a crashed aircraft. If it was, there might be survivors. In that freezing climate, there was no time to waste in getting help.

The Catalina climbed away from Spitzbergen, its radio operator flashing an urgent signal to the Norwegian Air-Sea Rescue Service. Within half an hour, rescue teams were on their way to the island by air. But as the Catalina flew homewards, its crew was unaware that their discovery on barren

Spitzbergen was destined to become one of the biggest mysteries of modern times.

A few days later, the Norwegian Government released an amazing statement to the newspapers. It claimed that the object found on the island was, incredibly, the wreck of a flying saucer – a disc-shaped craft that was definitely not of this earth. The statement also said that a thorough investigation and analysis of the alien object was being carried out by Norwegian, British and American experts. Journalists from all over the world flocked to Norway, seeking more information; but the Norwegian Government refused to make any further comment. After the initial earth-shaking announcement, there was only silence and complete secrecy.

The silence was broken very briefly a few months later, when an un-named United States Air Force spokesman told newsmen that the mystery craft had been of Soviet origin, and had carried Soviet markings. The newspapers were by no means satisfied but they filed the story as unusable through lack of reliable information and forgot about it.

Then, in September 1955, the Norwegian Government revealed that a Norwegian General Staff Board of Inquiry had practically completed an investigation into the nature of the mystery object, and was about to make its findings public. The Chairman of the Board, Norwegian Air Force Colonel Gernod Darnbyl, stated emphatically that the wrecked craft could not have originated on Earth. The materials used in its construction were completely unknown, and had defied every attempt at analysis. Therefore the statement that it was of Soviet origin was false. Furthermore, a detailed examination of the disc

had revealed certain technical features that were beyond the grasp of terrestrial science.

Colonel Darnbyl went on to say that a team of Air Force specialists – who had been keeping a close watch on the Arctic regions since the crashed disc was discovered – had formed the opinion that the area within the Arctic Circle was being used as a base by alien craft. The specialists had logged a great deal of UFO activity during their three years of surveillance. The statement concluded that the true facts behind the affair were of sensational importance, and should be made known to the public without delay. The full report would be published after discussions with the US and British Governments.

But the report was never published. One of Norway's NATO partners – either the USA or Britain, or maybe both – had apparently clamped down on the release of any further information. Both the USA and Britain, at that time, were classifying UFO information under the heading of "secret".

So the mystery of the Norwegian UFO remains. Was it really an alien spacecraft that was found

wrecked on Spitzbergen, and were its remains secretly spirited away to be examined behind locked doors? Or was there a more plausible, but equally secret, explanation behind what was found in the Arctic Circle?

Early in 1952, USAF reconnaissance aircraft were undertaking regular flights inside the Arctic Circle from bases in the United Kingdom. These aircraft, mainly giant Convair RB-36Ds, were gathering photographic intelligence on bases in the northern Soviet Union – and in particular on the island of Novaya Zemlya, where the Russians had built a new nuclear test centre.

One RB-36D is known to have been lost in 1952 while engaged on these clandestine missions. Was it its wreckage that was discovered on Spitzbergen – and was the flying-saucer story a deliberate invention to cover up the true details of what the Americans were doing? The question remains unanswered, but the fact remains that there are other cases where the wreckage of UFOs has allegedly been found, and the evidence rapidly removed.

● OPPOSITE Police examining an alleged UFO landing trace near Richmond, Virginia, on 21 April 1967.

● LEFT Ludvig Lindbäck, whose brother Knut witnessed the event, points to the spot in Lake Kölmjärv, Sweden, where a UFO crashed on 19 July 1946. The object was possibly a V-2 type rocket, test launched by the Russians from a captured German installation on the Baltic coast.

● BELOW The wreck of a crashed USAF B-36 bomber. Was it the remains of a secret reconnaissance version of this aircraft that was discovered on Spitzbergen?

The UFO in the Peropava River, Brazil

According to one account, a UFO that crashed in a river in South America may still be there. In the afternoon of 31 October, 1963, nine-year-old Ruth de Souza was playing with some young friends not far from her home on the banks of the Peropava River, in Brazil's Sao Paulo province, when she was startled by a strange roaring noise. Looking up into the sky, the children shrank back in fear. Moving slowly towards them at tree-top level was a shining disc, and it seemed to be losing height as it moved towards Ruth's house. Suddenly, there was a loud thud as the object collided with the trunk of a tall tree that stood in its path. The disc wavered, then changed course and moved out over the river, rocking violently. It seemed to be struggling to gain height. Then, abruptly, it plunged into the water like a stone and vanished. Mud and debris came bursting to the surface amid an explosion of huge bubbles. The river seemed to be boiling at the spot where the disc had disappeared.

Ruth's mother, Senōra Elidia Alves de Souza, had also been startled by the roaring sound. She came out of the house and ran to where the children were staring at the churning water. A minute later Ruth's uncle, Raul Alves also arrived at the scene. Like Elidia, he had heard the noise but had not seen the object. Utterly perplexed, he could give no answer to the children's questions. He drove to the nearby town of Iguape and reported the incident to the police. Although sceptical, they agreed to send officers to the scene.

Fortunately for the children – whose story might easily have been casually dismissed as a figment of childish imagination – some fishermen on the opposite bank of the river had also seen the flying disc. They said that the thing had been about three feet (1m) thick and between 15 and 20 feet (4.5 and 6m) in diameter. Somehow – perhaps because of its roar – they had got the impression that the disc was immensely powerful. It had been very

bright, like highly polished aluminium. Its movements had suggested to the fishermen that it was not manned, but was operated by some form of remote control.

The water at the point where the disc had crashed was about 12 feet (3.5m) deep, but beneath it was a 15-foot-thick (4.5m) layer of silt. The witnesses agreed that the disc had plunged into the water with sufficient force to bury itself deep in the mud. It had been heavy, too; the investigators found that a great gash had been torn in the trunk of the tree which the disc had struck during its erratic flight.

ABOVE AND RIGHT These remarkable pictures depict a UFO photographed over Trinidad Island in the South Atlantic on 16 January 1958. The UFO appears to have a flat disc encircling its main body.

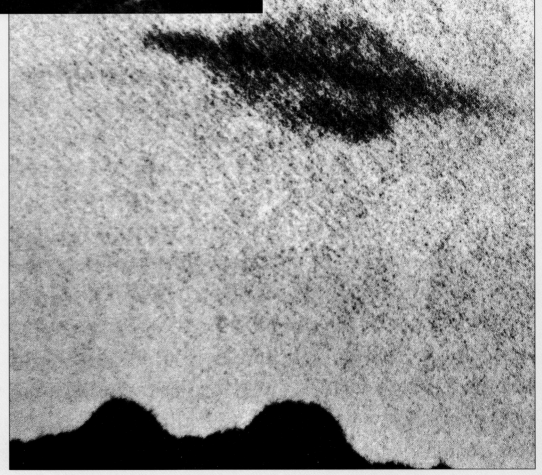

The police marked the exact spot where the disc had plunged into the river. By that same evening, every newspaper in Brazil had got hold of the story, and the following day hordes of curious sightseers and UFO investigators descended on the peaceful Peropava. Strangely enough – possibly because the disc had not come down in a military area – the Brazilian defence authorities showed no interest in the incident.

On the morning of 2 November, a diving instructor named Caetano Iovanne, with the assistance of two colleagues, made an attempt to recover the disc. For several hours they searched the murky river bed, probing here and there among the thick layer of mud, but they found no sign of the mystery object.

The next day, a second attempt was made by another team of divers, using special search equipment. They also drew a complete blank. All they succeeded in doing was to stir up large amounts of mud, which made conditions on the river-bed even more impossible than before.

Several more attempts were made over the next few days. Mine detectors were used to sweep the river-bed in the hope that they might reveal some trace of the metal object buried in the mud – but the thing had either sunk too deeply in the silt, or it had disappeared altogether. Someone suggested that it might have been washed downstream, but because of its perceived size and weight this was unlikely. Another theory was that it had moved downstream under its own power. If the disc really was some kind of spacecraft, it was even possible that it had been retrieved secretly during the night. Possible but improbable, for any activity would almost certainly have been seen.

The most likely conclusion is that the disc is still there, buried deep in the mud at the bottom of the Peropava. And the secret of its true origin will doubtless lie buried with it forever.

ABOVE Photographs of UFOs over the British Isles are comparatively rare. This one was snapped by Stephen Darbishire at Coniston in Cumbria's Lake District on 4 February 1954.

What the pilots saw

It was a beautiful night; the sky was crystal clear, with a full moon. In the streets, people looked up curiously as a roll of thunder split the warm stillness. High above their heads, four sets of twinkling navigation lights raced across the sky and vanished in the halo of radiance around the moon.

In the cockpit of the Portuguese Air Force F-84 Thunderjet there was complete silence, except for the muted whisper of the slipstream and the hum of electrical equipment. Captain José Ferreira was conscious of the beauty of the night too, but he had little time to enjoy it. He was preoccupied with the task of navigating his aircraft accurately.

● The cover of *Fate* magazine (left), dating from April 1957, shows a US jet fighter attacking a UFO. In reality, no such interception was ever made. Flying saucers featured heavily in the magazine during 1957. The depiction of a UFO encounter appeared on the front cover in August (below).

U.S. JET ATTACKS SAUCER !
TRUE STORIES OF THE STRANGE AND THE UNKNOWN
FATE ANC MAGAZINE
April 1957 35¢
I HAVE SEEN ZOMBIES

SAUCERS OVER EUROP
BY AIMÉ MICHEL
FATE ANC MAGAZINE
August 1957 35
ALL ABOARD FOR THE MOON
By FRANK EDWARDS

ABOVE A Republic F-84 Thunderjet, the type flown by Portuguese Air Force pilots when they had a frightening encounter with UFOs on the night of 4 September 1957 during a routine cross-country navigation exercise.

INSET This UFO was allegedly photographed by a bank employee in Warrington, Cheshire, in 1978. Defence departments in the USA and UK have been accused of "covering up" UFO reports; in fact, no such cover-up exists.

It had been 7.20pm on 4 September 1957, when Captain Ferreira and the three other Thunderjets of his flight had streaked down the runway of Ota Air Force Base, Portugal, on the first stage of a routine night cross-country navigation trip. The other three pilots were all sergeants: Manuel Marcelino, Alberto Covas and Alberto Oliveira. The four jets climbed steadily until they reached 25,000 feet (7,260m), then they levelled out and settled down on the flight towards their first turning-point, the Spanish town of Granada. Granada's lights twinkled on the horizon, right on schedule. Overhead, the four jets made a gentle turn until they were heading back towards the Portuguese border and their second checkpoint, the town of Portalegre.

It was then that Ferreira noticed something unusual – a brilliant, pulsating light away to port, hanging low over the horizon. The flight commander called up the other pilots; they had seen it, too. As they watched, the light seemed to glow with a multitude of colours: reds, blues and dazzling greens. Suddenly, it grew larger until it was about six times its original size; then, just as abruptly, it dwindled into a faint yellow pinpoint. Whatever it was, it seemed to be keeping pace with the Thunderjets.

At 10.35pm Captain Ferreira ordered his flight to abandon the planned exercise and execute a 50-degree turn to port. When the turn was completed, Ferreira looked for the mystery object, and saw that it had moved too. It was still directly over on his left, and it must have moved pretty fast to get there. There was now absolutely no doubt that the orange light was shadowing the F-84s.

The object, which was giving off a reddish glow, looked about the size of an orange. It was impossible to tell how far away it was. Although it was still keeping station with the jets, it had descended until it was well below their 25,000-foot (7,620m) altitude. For another 10 minutes, it followed the jets without changing its course, colour or size – and then, as the pilots watched, something incredible happened. One after the other, four small yellow discs broke away from the red object and took up an impeccable formation on either side of it.

All at once the red UFO, which appeared to be about fifteen times bigger than its companions, shot upwards in a fast climb straight towards the jets. Captain Ferreira shouted into his microphone, ordering his pilots to break formation. Opening his throttle, he pulled the Thunderjet around in a hard turn, trying to cross the path of the climbing UFO. In his windscreen, a point of light grew bigger with frightening speed. It was one of the smaller UFOs. It loomed up in Ferreira's gunsight, resolving itself into a flat disc. Instinctively, Ferreira jabbed his thumb down on the gun button, then remembered that the six machine guns of his Thunderjet were not armed. The next instant, the UFO sped overhead in a hazy blur and vanished.

Ferreira's earphones crackled with shouts as the other pilots desperately tried to avoid the hurtling UFOs. The discs were incredibly fast and manoeuvrable: no man-made object could move like that. The UFOs rocketed upwards in a vertical climb and disappeared in seconds. Breathing hard, Ferreira called up his excited pilots over the radio and brought his widely scattered flight back into formation. A few minutes later the pilots landed safely at their home base, shaken but none the worse for their uncanny encounter.

When the pilots' report was eventually released, a local weather observatory came up with an interesting piece of information. At precisely the time when Ferreira's pilots were tangling with the UFOs over the Portuguese border, the observatory's sensitive equipment had registered unaccountable variations in the Earth's magnetic field – a common occurrence in areas where UFOs are sighted.

Captain Ferreira and his pilots were convinced that the objects they had seen were not of this world. And later, when Ferreira was telling his story to Portuguese Air Force investigators, he said: "Please don't come out with the old explanation that we were being chased by the planet Venus, weather balloons, or freak atmospheric conditions. Whatever we saw up there was real, and intelligently controlled. And it scared the hell out of us."

> **"Please don't come out with the old explanation that we were being chased by the planet Venus, weather balloons, or freak atmospheric conditions. Whatever we saw up there was real, and intelligently controlled. And it scared the hell out of us."**

Sightings by RAF and USAF personnel in the UK

A similar occurrence, this time in daylight, also frightened Flight Lieutenant J. R. Salandin of the Royal Air Force on 4 October 1954. In fact, he was so shaken by his experience that he had to fly around for a further 10 minutes before he could pull himself together sufficiently to tell Control what he had seen.

Salandin, a pilot with No. 111 Squadron, RAF Fighter Command, had taken off from North Weald in Essex in his Gloster Meteor jet fighter at 4.15pm. Climbing towards two other aircraft which he could see above him, he was surprised to see two small objects, one silvery and the other gold, pass nearby. Salandin had hardly recovered from his surprise and was still wondering whether he had been the victim of a hallucination when he happened to look straight ahead – and received one of the biggest frights of his flying career.

Straight towards him at tremendous speed was a disc-shaped object. In the brief time Salandin had for observation, the thing appeared to have a flange in the centre and two bulges above and below this. It was so near that it overlapped his windscreen. A collision seemed inevitable. Then, at the last moment, the object swerved and flashed past on the Meteor's port side.

There have been a number of instances where UFOs have been recorded on the gun-camera film of fighter aircraft. The camera is activated when the pilot presses the firing button and, as well as in actual combat, is used to record "kills" during simulated dogfights. The Operations Record Book of No. 43 Squadron RAF tells of one incident in 1955, when two Hawker Hunter jet fighters were engaged in mock combat high over the North Sea. When the gun-camera film of the attacking Hunter was screened at the exercise de-briefing, it showed a ball of bright light, that appeared to be solid, drifting slowly into the frame. The ball hung there for several moments, appearing to be pacing the two aircraft, and remained poised about half-way between them before drifting away again. Neither pilot had seen anything.

BELOW This UFO was photographed at 12,000 ft (3,657m) by Shinichi Takeda of Fujisaw, Japan. The object appeared to be shadowing the airliner in which the photographer was travelling.

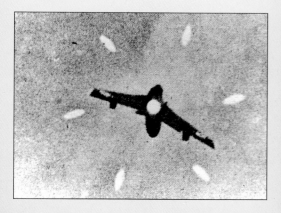

ABOVE A Hawker Hunter jet fighter of RAF Fighter Command is captured in the gunsight of another during a combat exercise. On one occasion in 1955, a UFO appeared on the gun-camera film of a Hunter dogfighting over the North Sea.

The Royal Air Force never paid a great deal of attention to UFO sightings; they were duly recorded in squadron operations record books, and sometimes became the subject of "special occurrence reports", but that was all. Not unnaturally, the Air Ministry (Ministry of Defence (RAF) from 1960)

LEFT The elongated fuselage of an aircraft in flight can sometimes be mistaken for a UFO under certain light conditions. It would not be difficult, for example, for these B-36 bombers to appear as something out of the ordinary at a distance. The B-36 served with the USAF at the height of the "flying saucer" era.

BELOW A de Havilland Venom night-fighter, the type that chased a UFO over much of East Anglia on the night of 13 August 1956. The Venom's radar operator reported that the UFO was capable of fantastic speeds.

received frequent requests from members of the public, asking for information about the UFO phenomenon; the official line was one of "no comment", simply because there was no firm evidence to comment on. This led to speculation that the ministry was involved in some sort of dark and sinister "cover-up", but in reality there was never anything of the sort.

Neither was there a deliberate cover-up in the United States, where the whole UFO question was treated far more seriously by the USAF. Although UFO sightings were given a "secret" classification for many years, at the height of the Cold War, so were many other happenings involving the military.

The USAF's investigation into UFO sightings by both military and civilian pilots was carried out in a programme code-named Project Sign, which was downgraded in 1949 and its name changed to Project Grudge. In 1951 the name was changed yet again, this time to Project Blue Book, and its coverage expanded to include all UFO sightings. By the end of 1953 more than 4,000 sightings had been logged, but about half these were very unreliable and the Blue Book investigators evolved a system whereby witnesses were graded according to age,

observational experience and so forth. Reports from pilots naturally continued to receive high priority, and there were plenty of them.

One extraordinary case, on 13 August 1956, involved a joint effort between the USAF and RAF in an attempt to intercept a UFO. At 9.30pm, radar operators in the Ground Controlled Approach (GCA) unit at the USAF base of Bentwaters, near Ipswich in Suffolk, detected something odd about 30 miles (48km) out over the North Sea. It was heading inland, and closing at a phenomenal speed, covering six miles (9.5km) with every four-second sweep of the radar antenna. The incredulous controllers worked out its velocity at close on 5,000 miles per hour (8,000kmh). At the same time, more radar targets were picked up at a range of 8 miles (13km), also moving towards Bentwaters. Between 12 and 15 echoes were approaching in a cluster, preceded by three more objects in triangular formation. The pilot of a Lockheed T-33 jet trainer belonging to the 512th Fighter Intercepter Wing at Soesterberg in the Netherlands, who was heading for Bentwaters on a night navigational sortie, was asked to investigate but saw nothing.

The cluster continued its passage, increasing the range to around 40 miles (64km), then merged to form a single, very powerful radar echo. It remained stationary for nearly 15 minutes, moved

off to the north-east, stopped again for a few minutes, then gathered speed and vanished from the radar scope.

The original, single radar target, meanwhile, had merged with ground echoes and been lost. But at ten o'clock another single blip – or perhaps it was the same one – appeared on Bentwaters' radar, crossing the screen at an estimated 4,000mph (6,400kmh). A strange object was also detected on radar at nearby Lakenheath, also a USAF base in Suffolk. HQ 3rd Air Division, controlling all USAF units in Britain, was alerted, and so was RAF Fighter Command, which was responsible for the air defence of the British Isles. The alert now passed to the RAF Ground Controlled Interception (GCI) radar complex at Neatishead, Norfolk, about 40 miles (64km) north-east of Lakenheath. The GCI controller there was authorized to scramble an interceptor.

That night, it was the turn of No. 253 Squadron of the RAF's No. 11 Group to man the night-fighter "battle flight" in East Anglia, with the crew – pilot and radar observer – of a de Havilland Venom NF.2 strapped in their cockpit and ready to scramble at a moment's notice. When the call came, the Venom was quickly airborne and heading towards the target detected by Lakenheath radar. Meanwhile, at RAF Waterbeach, No. 253 Squadron's base, a second Venom night-fighter crew was brought to cockpit readiness.

The radar operator in the first Venom established contact with the UFO and steered the pilot on a course to intercept. The target was now stationary, and the Venom rapidly came within gun range – at which point the radar operator lost contact. It was hardly surprising: both Lakenheath and Neatishead informed the Venom crew that the UFO was now behind them and keeping pace with them as their aircraft circled.

For the best part of 10 minutes the Venom pilot did his best to shake off the UFO, but it clung doggedly to his tail, remaining at a distance of about 200 yards (180m). In the end, the pilot broke away and headed back towards Waterbeach; the UFO followed him for a while, then stopped. It eventually began to move again, heading north at 600mph (965km), and vanished from Lakenheath's radar screens at a range of about 60 miles (96km). The Second Venom was scrambled, but its crew never made contact with the mystery object.

Huge flying walnut between Iceland and Japan

What occurred over East Anglia that night remains just as much a puzzle as the strange object that shadowed a Japan Airlines Boeing 747 freighter for 30 minutes in January 1988. The 747 was flying from Iceland to Japan via Alaska when its crew sighted the object, which was described by the aircraft captain, Kenju Terauchi, as "very big, about twice the size of an aircraft carrier". He said that it closed to within five miles (8km) of the aircraft, and asked US air-traffic controllers for permission to take evasive action if necessary. The controllers confirmed the existence of a large blip on their radar screens, and said that it might have been composed of three separate objects flying close together. To the 747 crew, it looked like a huge flying walnut. The US Federal Aviation Administration launched an investigation, but came up with no answers.

● BELOW This photograph is an enlargement of the mystery object that appeared to shadow a Martin B-57 jet bomber during a test flight from Edwards Air Force Base, California, in September 1957.

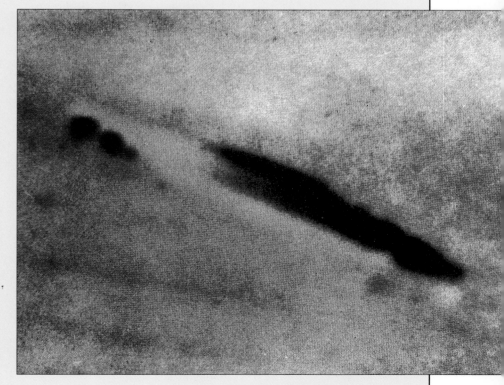

UFOs in history

The search for UFO sightings, or evidence that alien space travellers have visited Earth in ancient times, covers a very broad canvas and has given rise to some startling claims. Sodom and Gomorrah were destroyed by alien spacecraft launching nuclear missiles; the walls of Jericho were knocked down by ultrasonic sound waves beamed down from on high; the Great Pyramid was designed with the help of advanced information supplied by extra-terrestrial engineers, and so on.

The ancient site of Nazca, Peru

One of the favourite hunting-grounds for "evidence" of extra-terrestrial visits is Peru, and in particular the ancient site near Nazca, where patterns of strange lines cover an area of 200 square miles (518km^2) between the Pacific Ocean and the Andes Mountains. First discovered by Spanish explorers in the 16th century, the lines spread out in all directions, carved into the rocky surfaces. They depict all manner of geometric shapes, intermingled with huge drawings of animal figures including birds, a spider, a lizard, a snake, a whale, a monkey and a llama. There is also the figure of a man with a halo. Some of the figures are over 900 feet (275m) long, others less than 100 feet (30m).

Serious investigation into the lines began about 50 years ago, when airline pilots started to use them for navigation. Archaeologists travelled to Peru to survey the lines, and to find out more about the long-dead civilization that had carved them into the landscape. The Nazca Indians were a race who inhabited Peru 2,000 years ago, before the Incas – but no one knows for certain whether they carved the lines, or whether they were formed by an even earlier race. The patterns could be as much as 8,000 years old.

According to UFO addicts, the purpose of the curious lines is clear; they formed a kind of navigational beacon that enabled alien spacecraft to home in on Peru when they visited the Nazcas, their occupants imparting much valuable know-

ledge to the natives. The latest theory, advanced by modern science, is much more plausible: the lines were designed as an astronomical calendar, the figures aligned to predict the annual positions of the sun, moon, planets and stars. They were used to predict the correct time of year for planting seeds, harvesting crops and the appearance of water each year in the region's rivers. In this respect, they served the purpose supposed to be the reason for Britain's Stonehenge.

The intriguing aspect, however, is how the intricate patterns were surveyed in the first place, and how the ancient designers were able to retain a fantastic degree of accuracy over great distances. The lines can only be seen in their true perspective from the air, a fact that has long sustained the UFO theory. But lately, scientists have put forward a new notion: the ancient surveyors may have built and flown primitive hot-air balloons. This idea was first projected by an American scientific team, investigating some odd pits that lay close to the end of the lines. The circular pits were blackened by fire, and were just about the right diameter to fit the base of a Montgolfier-type hot-air balloon. Investigating further, the scientists took another look at scraps of linen found in Nazcan tombs, and found that the weave was much tighter than that of the material used to make the envelopes of 18th-century balloons. So the researchers decided to build their own balloon, using the materials the Nazcans might have used, including reeds to build the gondola, to find out if the idea worked.

To their amazement the project was successful. The balloon, designed by American Bill Spohrer, was launched from one of the burn-pits carrying two passengers, Jim Woodman and Julian Knott, both experienced balloonists. Named Condor I, the balloon rose to a height of about 100 feet (30m), but then a sudden downdraught brought it close to the ground again and the two occupants jumped out, thinking it was going to crash. Luckily neither was hurt, and the balloon rose again to a height of over 1,000 feet (300m) and flew for nearly two miles (3km) before coming to earth.

Sadly, no one has been able to prove conclusively that this was the technique originally used to survey the Nazca lines. But the intriguing possibility remains that the ancient Peruvians may have been the first men to learn to fly – with or without extraterrestrial advice.

The so-called "Nazca Lines" in Peru have baffled scientists for many years. First discovered by Spanish explorers in the 16th century, they depict all manner of geometric shapes intermingled with huge drawings of animal figures. The patterns, it is thought, could only have been aligned through aerial observation, and one theory is that the ancient race that carved them used primitive hot-air balloons. According to UFO devotees, the lines formed a kind of navigational beacon that enabled alien spacecraft to home in on Peru in the distant past.

Out of place artefacts

A continuing underlying theme behind alleged alien contact with Earth in ancient times is the advanced knowledge that some ancient civilizations appear to have possessed. Ever since archaeologists first dug their spades into ancient sites, they have been turning up strange objects that cannot be explained – objects bearing an uncanny resemblance to items that can only be produced by modern technology.

And because they could not be explained rationally such objects have since been tucked away in the dark recesses of museums all over the world, forgotten by everyone except a handful of writers who have tried to prove that they are the remnants of long-lost civilizations. Scientists know them as OOPARTS – Out Of Place Artefacts – and are today attempting to solve their mysteries once and for all.

BELOW This object, drawn in 1493 by Hermann Schaden, bears an uncanny resemblance to the black monolith in the film of Arthur C. Clark's science fiction novel, *2001 – A Space Odyssey*, and its sequel, *2010*.

LEFT This artefact, discovered in Iraq near Baghdad in 1936, is said to be a 1,800-year-old electric cell. When tested by scientists, it produced a current of up to two volts.

Already, investigators have come up with some astonishing results. In 1936, for example, archaeologists unearthed a strange object from the ruins of a village near Baghdad; it was a clay jar, containing a cylinder of sheet copper with an iron rod suspended in its centre. Since then, similar objects have been found at other sites in Iraq. The original jar and its contents were put on display in the Cairo Museum, Egypt. On several occasions, people who saw it remarked that it looked just like an electric cell. Proof again, said the Ufologists, of technical knowledge passed on by space travellers.

Oddly enough, no one tried to prove that it could be an electric cell until 1976, when a team of German scientists from Hildesheim built an exact replica and, as an acid substitute, filled it with grape juice. There was no longer any doubt that it was an electric battery, for it produced a current of up to two volts in strength. Yet the original battery may be as much as 2,000 years old. So where did the ancient race who lived near what is now Baghdad obtain the knowledge to build it, and for what purpose was it used?

No one, as yet, can answer the first question, but the Germans think they might have an answer to the second. In an experiment, they immersed a small silver statue in a gold cyanide solution and passed an electric current from their model battery through it. In just a couple of hours, the process had given the statue a thin layer of gold. The inference is that ancient goldsmiths used electric current to electroplate their valuables.

Another mysterious object the scientists have worked on is a strange mechanism found in the wreck of a Greek merchant ship that sank in the Aegean sea about 80 BC. Made of bronze and encased in wood, it split into four fragments when it dried out, and the inner surfaces of these fragments were found to contain small, delicate wheels. For a long time, it was thought that the mechanism – discovered in 1900 – was part of an ancient astrolabe, used to calculate the angle of the sun and other celestial bodies. Then, in 1971, scientists investigating the mechanism at America's Yale University took a series of gamma- and X-radiographs of the strange object, and these showed internal details which had not been seen before.

It appeared that the object was not a simple astrolabe, but something far more advanced. It was

a miniature planetarium, using some 30 gears of varying sizes and employing a differential gear system which allowed two shafts to rotate at different speeds. It was to be a thousand years after that Greek ship went down before differential gears were re-invented in the Western world.

In terms of time, that is nothing. Scientists have just discovered that strange markings, carved on bone tools found throughout Europe, represent the phases of the moon – not just as they were when primitive man observed them, but as they would be when the seasons changed. Those bone tools are 30,000 years old, which has led to a drastic revision of scientific thinking about when man first began to observe the heavens, and record what he saw.

There is also the more famous case of the Saqqara Bird. A wooden bird-like object about five and a half inches (14cm) long, it was discovered among the contents of an Egyptian tomb in 1891 and dated to 200 BC. Recently, aero-engineers have carried out a series of tests on it, and they have reached the conclusion that whoever built it, whether as a child's toy or the model for some bigger craft that was never built, must have had a considerable knowledge of aeronautics. The object's wings and fuselage show aerodynamic characteristics and refinements that could not have been stumbled upon accidentally by someone just setting out to carve a toy bird. And it flies, too – perfectly, just like a model glider.

The question is, if the ancient Egyptians had the knowledge to build a model glider such as this, why did they not progress to build a full-size flying-machine? A possible answer is that they might have done, and we don't know about it. Unfortunately, most of the knowledge of the ancient world was stored in the famous library of Alexandria, and

BELOW LEFT A man-built "UFO" in Chinese history: the flying chariot of Ki Kung. This illustration dates from the Sung Dynasty (990-179 AD). The idea is probably based on the man-carrying kites that were used by the Chinese for observation purposes during this period.

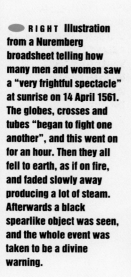

RIGHT Illustration from a Nuremberg broadsheet telling how many men and women saw a "very frightful spectacle" at sunrise on 14 April 1561. The globes, crosses and tubes "began to fight one another", and this went on for an hour. Then they all fell to earth, as if on fire, and faded slowly away producing a lot of steam. Afterwards a black spearlike object was seen, and the whole event was taken to be a divine warning.

lost forever when this was burned down by the Romans in AD 391. Parts of the library had been destroyed before, but on this occasion its greatest treasure – its priceless manuscript collection – was wiped out.

Some scientists believe that the lost knowledge may have held the answer to another big puzzle: how the ancients managed to move huge blocks of stone hundreds of miles to build their great monuments. Recent scientific investigation has shown that the molecular structure of some stones has been altered, leading to the theory that ancient civilizations may have known how to liquify them by chemical means, turning them into a kind of plastic for ease of transportation and then reconstituting them in moulds at the building site. The idea is not entirely fanciful. The Huanca Indians of Bolivia still make stone objects by liquifying rock on a small scale with oxalic acid, extracted from rhubarb leaves and other plants. Perhaps the process they use is a dim memory of a much greater one, used on a world-wide scale thousands of years ago.

These are just a few examples of the degree of knowledge that was apparently possessed by the ancient world, and subsequently lost. The question of whether fabled civilizations such as that of Atlantis, armed with vast scientific knolwedge, really existed, is outside the scope of this book. But supposing they did, where did their knowledge come from? The legends of the ancients are filled with tales of flying-machines and other things which equate with our present state of knowledge; it is, perhaps, stretching the imagination a little too far to believe that mankind could have reached such an advanced stage of technical development, unaided, many thousands of years ago.

The main difficulty in analysing this matter, especially in the context of possible extra-terrestrial contact, is to divide tenuous fact – or at least reasonable supposition – from obvious fiction. Many of the "ancient texts", purporting to provide references to such contact, simply never existed; they were the invention of 20th-century writers. Or, if some sort of basic text did exist, it was deliberately doctored to convey the impression that it referred in part to UFO sightings, weapons of mass destruction and so on. It may be that the key to the mystery of whether Earth was visited by extra-terrestrials at the dawn of history lies waiting to be discovered. But it will take a mighty scientific wind of discovery to blow away the smokescreen that has been laid over the years by unscrupulous charlatans.